Language Literacy Lessons
Writing
Elementary

by Imogene Forte

Incentive Publications, Inc.
Nashville, Tennessee

Illustrated by Gayle S. Harvey
Cover Art by Becky Rüegger
Edited by Jean K. Signor

ISBN 0-86530-573-0

PRINTED IN THE UNITED STATES OF AMERICA
www.incentivepublications.com

Table of Contents

Composition and Creative Writing 43

HOW TO USE THIS BOOK

Achieving language literacy is a major benchmark in the education of every student in today's classrooms. Without reading, writing, speaking, and listening literacy the process of learning becomes increasingly difficult and the limits placed on academic achievement become more entrenched and solidified each year.

In the information saturated and technology dependent world of today, it is especially important for children to gain and be able to make meaningful use of the skills associated with language literacy at an early age. Success in content-based studies such as Math, Social Studies, and Science, and even in enrichment fields including Art, Music, and Literature are highly dependent on language literacy proficiency. With strong language skills, a student's academic future has fewer bounds and individual goals, expectancies and dreams stand a better chance of being realized. It was with respect for the importance of achieving a high level of language literacy for every student that the Language Literacy Lessons Series was developed.

The purpose of *Language Literacy Lessons: Writing, Elementary* is to help students achieve the desired literacy milestone through reinforcement of key language skills. The activities in this book have all been designed to provide student practice of essential writing skills. A skills checklist on page 10 details the skills covered. This skills checklist has been carefully gleaned from attention to research related to language, while specific skills associated with each lesson are correlated to the age-appropriate language literacy checklist.

Through the use of the lessons in this book, students will be advancing individual language literacy skills while working toward national standards! For help in lesson planning, an easy-to-use matrix on pages 8 and 9 presents National Language Arts Standards correlations for each lesson in the book.

Not only are the activities correlated to essential literacy skills and National Language Arts Standards, they are imaginative and their open-ended nature will prove to be engaging and of high-interest to students. Student creativity is tapped through intriguing situations to write about, interesting characters to read about, and captivating illustrations to inspire thoughtful student responses.

As language literacy skills improve, increased levels of overall school success will be readily apparent. Language literacy enables students to set achievable goals to go wherever their interests take them and to embark joyfully on a lifelong journey of learning!

STANDARDS MATRIX

STANDARD	ACTIVITY PAGE
Standard 1: Students read a wide range of print and nonprint text to build an understanding of texts, of themselves, and of the cultures of the United States and the world, to acquire new information, to respond to the needs and demands of society and the workplace, and for personal fulfillment. Among these texts are fiction and nonfiction, classic and contemporary works.	17, 18, 23, 68, 73, 75
Standard 2: Students read a wide range of literature from many periods in many genres to build an understanding of the many dimensions (e.g., philosophical, ethical, aesthetic) of human experience.	21, 26, 45, 46, 47, 72
Standard 3: Students apply a wide range of strategies to comprehend, interpret, evaluate, and appreciate texts. They draw on their prior experience, their interactions with other readers and writers, their knowledge of word meaning and of other texts, their identification strategies, and their understanding of textual features (e.g., sound-letter correspondence, sentence structure, context, graphics).	12–18, 23, 31, 33, 35, 48, 59
Standard 4: Students adjust their use of spoken, written, and visual language (e.g., conventions, style, vocabulary) to communicate effectively with a variety of audiences for a variety of purposes.	19–23, 32, 55–57, 58, 60, 61, 62, 66
Standard 5: Students employ a wide range of strategies as they write and use different writing process elements appropriately to communicate with different audiences for a variety of purposes.	29, 32, 38, 40, 48, 63, 64, 65, 77
Standard 6: Students apply knowledge of language structure, language conventions (e.g., spelling and punctuation), media techniques, figurative language, and genre to create, critique, and discuss print and non-print texts.	24, 25-30, 31, 34, 39, 69

Language Literacy Lessons / Writing Elementary Copyright ©2002 by Incentive Publications, Inc. Nashville, TN.

STANDARDS MATRIX

STANDARD	ACTIVITY PAGE
Standard 7: Students conduct research on issues and interests by generating ideas and questions, and by posing problems. They gather, evaluate, and synthesize data from a variety of sources (e.g., print and non-print texts, artifacts, people) to communicate their discoveries in ways that suit their purpose and audience.	51, 67, 71, 72, 74
Standard 8: Students use a variety of technological and informational resources (e.g., libraries, databases, computer networks, video) to gather and synthesize information and to create and communicate knowledge.	36, 40, 44, 69
Standard 9: Students develop an understanding of and respect for diversity in language use, patterns, and dialects across cultures, ethnic groups, geographic regions, and social roles.	45, 46, 53, 71
Standard 10: Students whose first language is not English make use of their first language to develop competency in the English language arts and to develop understanding of content across the curriculum.	30, 41, 55–58, 70
Standard 11: Students participate as knowledgeable, reflective, creative, and critical members of a variety of literacy communities.	49, 50, 52–53
Standard 12: Students use spoken, written, and visual language to accomplish their own purposes (e.g., for learning, enjoyment, persuasion, and the exchange of information).	19, 36, 37, 42, 54, 61, 62, 76

Language Literacy Lessons / Writing Elementary
Copyright ©2002 by Incentive Publications, Inc.
Nashville, TN.

Standards for the English Language Arts, by the International Reading Association and the National Council of Teachers of English, Copyright 1996 by the International Reading Association and the National Council of Teachers of English. Reprinted with permission.

SKILLS CHECKLIST

	SKILL	PAGE
	Identify and use nouns	12–14, 16
	Identify and use verbs	15, 16
	Identify and use adverbs	17
	Identify and use adjectives	18
	Using descriptive words	19, 20
	Using homonyms	21
	Using antonyms	22
	Internalizing word meanings and clichés	23
	Using abbreviations	24
	Spelling	25
	Using punctuation marks	26–28, 34
	Writing four kinds of sentences	29
	Writing complete sentences	30, 32
	Correcting run-on sentences	31
	Sequencing thoughts	33, 35, 48
	Organizing and writing a paragraph	36–42
	Descriptive writing	36, 42, 54
	Who, What, When, Where, and Why	44
	Writing a biography	45, 46
	Writing an autobiography	47
	Writing directions	48, 64, 65
	Writing questions	49, 50
	Writing riddles	51
	Writing a letter	52, 53
	Writing dialogue	55–57
	Developing plot for a play	58
	Writing rhymed couplets	59
	Writing an acrostic	60
	Writing a haiku	61
	Creating a poster	62
	Writing a short imaginative piece	63, 68, 69, 72, 73, 75, 76, 77
	Writing a product description	66
	Generate and organize ideas for writing	67, 70, 71, 72, 74

Vocabulary Development
and
Technical Writing Skills

A Midnight Journey

A **noun** is the name of a person, place, or thing.

The ship will set sail at midnight. The Captain needs to organize the nouns for the journey ahead.

Read the nouns on the ship.

Decide if each noun names a person, place, or thing.

Write each noun on the correct sail.

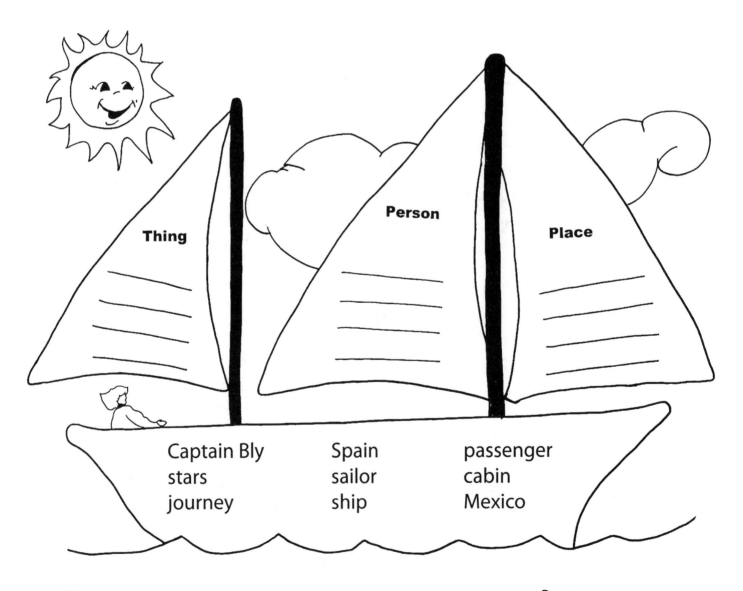

Name: _____

Date: _____

Using Nouns

Language Literacy Lessons / Writing Elementary
Copyright ©2002 by Incentive Publications, Inc.
Nashville, TN.

Name the Characters

Names are **proper nouns.** They always begin with a capital letter.

Kelly asked friends to play parts in the play she wrote, but she forgot to write their names correctly. Study the pictures of the different characters.

Write the name of each person under the character they will play.

brenda will play the part of Cheerful Clara.
sid will play the part of Grumpy Gus.
Lazy Louise will be played by chris.
henry will have the part of Sad Sam.
betina will have the role of Shy Sue.
Happy Harriette will be played by jean.

Brenda

Lazy Luuise

Grumpy Gus

Happy Harriette

henry

Name: _____ Date: _____

Language Literacy Lessons / Writing Elementary
Copyright ©2002 by Incentive Publications, Inc.
Nashville, TN.

Proper Nouns

Flowers A-Plenty

A plural noun names **more than one** of something.

Find and circle the names of the following flowers in the word find puzzle.

As you find and circle each flower, write the plural form of it in the space provided.

Crocus _____   Iris _____   Poppy _____

Rose _____   Lilac _____   Lily _____

Tulip _____   Orchid _____   Pansy _____

Daisy _____   Violet _____

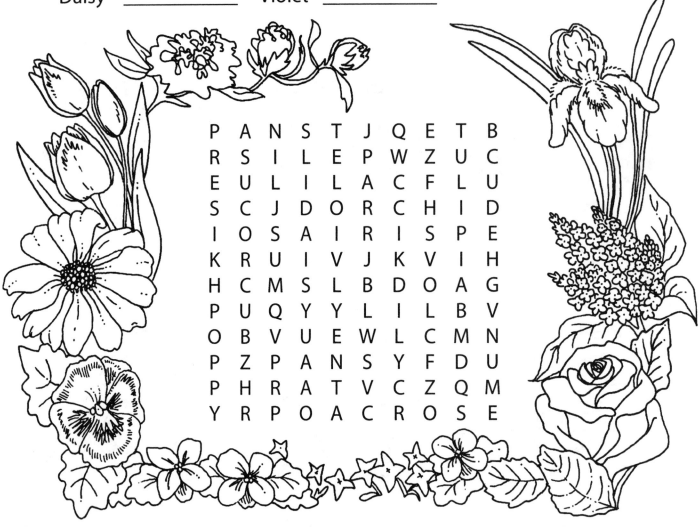

```
P A N S T J Q E T B
R S I L E P W Z U C
E U L I L A C F L U
S C J D O R C H I D
I O S A I R I S P E
K R U I V J K V I H
H C M S L B D O A G
P U Q Y Y L I L B V
O B V U E W L C M N
P Z P A N S Y F D U
P H R A T V C Z Q M
Y R P O A C R O S E
```

Name: _____   Date: _____

Plural Nouns

Language Literacy Lessons / Writing Elementary
Copyright ©2002 by Incentive Publications, Inc.
Nashville, TN.

Verbs on the Move

A **verb** shows action.

Write 3 verbs that show some action that would be possible for each of the nouns pictured below. Use your dictionary if you need spelling help.

Language Literacy Lessons / Writing Elementary
Copyright ©2002 by Incentive Publications, Inc.
Nashville, TN.

Action Verbs

Trace the Cottage Path

Trace the path through the forest.

Color in all the spaces that contain a word that can be used as both a noun and a verb.

Name:

Date:

Nouns and Verbs

Language Literacy Lessons / Writing Elementary
Copyright ©2002 by Incentive Publications, Inc.
Nashville, TN.

Scrambled Adverbs

An **adverb** describes a verb. It tells when, where, or how something happened.

Adverb Annie has some mixed-up adverbs for you to find.

Unscramble the adverbs in the word box to find the correct word to complete each sentence below.

The day for the class picnic had _ _ _ _ _ _ _ arrived. (allinfy)

The boys and girls hustled _ _ _ _ _ _ _ _ _ about as they _ _ _ _ _ _ _
prepared for the big event. (eefllyuchr)

_ _ _ _ _ _ _ , they began to pack the lunch. (aphpyli)

_ _ _ _ _ , they put the sandwiches in the basket. (rsift)

The chips were _ _ _ _ to go in. (xent)

The salad was then placed _ _ _ _ _ _ _ _ _ so that
it would not get crushed. (ercallyuf)

_ _ _ _ of all, the cookies and cakes were added. (alts)

_ _ _ _ _ _ _ _ _ they closed the basket (xcedityle)
and _ _ _ _ _ _ _ _ _ rushed out the door. (feelgyllu)

Scrambled
Word List:
aphpyli
qlcyuik
xent
rsift
allinfy
xcedityle
feelgyllu
alts
ercallyuf
eefllyuchr

Language Literacy Lessons / Writing Elementary
Copyright ©2002 by Incentive Publications, Inc.
Nashville, TN.

Adverbs

A Day At the Zoo

Adjectives are used to help readers see a person, place, or thing as the writer sees it.

The writer of the paragraph below used too many adjectives.

Rewrite the paragraph using fewer adjectives to make the paragraph clearer and more interesting.

> The zoo was a wonderful, noisy, exciting place. The funny monkeys, with their frisky but simple expressions, were always delightful. There were cages full of fancy, beautiful, delicate birds of every color and size. On one side were the wild animals—ferocious-looking lions, big, burly bears, and some of the tallest giant giraffes imaginable. Of course, one of the best things about the zoo was seeing the baby animals. The cute, soft baby ducks and the adorable, friendly lambs seemed so glad to see us. A day at the zoo was the nicest, most pleasant way to spend a bright sunny Sunday afternoon.

_____

_____

_____

_____

_____

_____

_____

_____

_____

Name: _____   Date: _____

Adjectives

Language Literacy Lessons / Writing Elementary
Copyright ©2002 by Incentive Publications, Inc.
Nashville, TN.

Creature Feature

Use your crayons to color this creature.

Write 5 words to describe the creature.

Use the words to write a story about it.

Leave the title line blank until your story is complete. Then read the story and give it a title.

1. _____

2. _____

3. _____

4. _____

5. _____

Title:

_____

_____

_____

_____

_____

_____

_____

_____

_____

_____

Name: _____   Date: _____

Descriptive Words

What Happened?

Here is a house.

This is the same house only one year later.

What do you think could have happened to the house in just one year?

_____

Fill the roof of each house with ten or more descriptive words that tell how it looks or makes you feel.

Name: _____ Date: _____

Descriptive Words

Language Literacy Lessons / Writing Elementary
Copyright ©2002 by Incentive Publications, Inc.
Nashville, TN.

Homonym Hikers

A **homonym** is a word that is pronounced the same as another word but is spelled differently and has a different meaning.

Fill in the blanks below with the correct homonym.

1. On the first day of their camping trip, Mr. Worthington and his _____ Tommy woke up early to watch the _____ rise.

2. They were hungry and, after cooking some eggs and _____ pieces of bacon, they _____ breakfast.

3. Then they felt ready to hike up a nearby mountain so they could _____ the _____ below.

4. They had heard a _____ about a sea monster that had a twenty-foot-long _____.

5. They made a bet about whether the monster would appear, but by _____ o'clock Tommy gave up and said his dad had _____ the bet. He said he didn't want to _____ any longer, and he said they would lose _____ if they didn't eat lunch soon!

sun, son   tale, tail

eight, ate   won, one

sea, see   wait, weight

Name: _____   Date: _____

Language Literacy Lessons / Writing Elementary
Copyright ©2002 by Incentive Publications, Inc.
Nashville, TN.

Homonyms

A Parrot's Luck

In this story about a parrot, you will find 7 underlined words.

Copy the story on the lines below, changing each underlined word by writing a word that has the opposite meaning.

Select the words needed from the word list, then finish the story.

Word List:

evening	dark
week	table
trip	black
walk	quiet
country	moonlight
read	night
bark	

A Day in the Sunlight

One morning, Polly Parrot realized that she was in the city. She wondered if she was having a dream. It was very light outside, and everything was noisy. Polly wanted to go out. She put on her white coat and headed for the door.

_____

_____

_____

_____

_____

_____

_____

_____

Name: _____   Date: _____

Antonyms

Language Literacy Lessons / Writing Elementary
Copyright ©2002 by Incentive Publications, Inc.
Nashville, TN.

Clichés on the Line

Some expressions are used so often that they become boring.

Each of the following sentences contains such an expression.

Write a sentence telling what you think each underlined phrase means.

1. I <u>heaved a sigh of relief</u> when the roller-coaster ride was over.

_____

2. My pencil must have <u>vanished into thin air</u>.

_____

3. Sometimes my brother <u>burns the midnight oil</u>.

_____

4. It <u>dawned on me</u> that it was my mother's birthday.

_____

5. <u>As the crow flies</u>, Ed's house is 5 minutes from my house.

_____

6. I like <u>each and every one</u> of my brother's friends.

_____

7. The haunted house left me <u>at a loss for words</u>.

_____

Name: _____

Date: _____

Language Literacy Lessons / Writing Elementary
Copyright ©2002 by Incentive Publications, Inc.
Nashville, TN.

Clichés

Abbreviated Touchdown

When Obal, from the planet Grindal, landed his spaceship on Earth, he sent back a report to the fleet commander.

Read Obal's computer report, and circle all the abbreviations in it.

Then write the abbreviations from his report and all the words they represent on the computer printout below.

To: Gen. Rebloh   From: Capt. Obal

Grindal Spaceship No. 426 touched down on planet Earth at 2:00 a.m. on Tues., Mar. 8, at 641 St. Augusta Ave. in Dallas, TX. Most creatures we see are 6 ft. tall, walk on two legs, and wear big hats. We have been here for one hr. and 18 min., and must stop communication now. A follow-up report will be sent later this p.m.

Computer Printout

Abbreviation	Word
1. _____	_____
2. _____	_____
3. _____	_____
4. _____	_____
5. _____	_____
6. _____	_____
7. _____	_____
8. _____	_____
9. _____	_____
10. _____	_____
11. _____	_____
12. _____	_____
13. _____	_____

Language Literacy Lessons / Writing Elementary
Copyright ©2002 by Incentive Publications, Inc.
Nashville, TN.

Spelling Bee

Good writers need to be good spellers.

Fill this spelling bee's wings with words you can spell.

Use some nouns, some pronouns,
some verbs, and some adjectives.

Name:

Date:

Language Literacy Lessons / Writing Elementary
Copyright ©2002 by Incentive Publications, Inc.
Nashville, TN.

Spelling

A Lamb's Tale

Read the story below.

Write 3 sentences to complete the story. Then supply the correct punctuation for the entire story.

Once upon a time long long ago a wooly white lamb was owned by a little girl named Mary The lamb had a very bad habit of following Mary to school each day To tell the truth Mary liked having the lamb at school but the teacher had a different opinion

Oh no not again the teacher would say Mary why did you bring that lamb to school

Please teacher Mary would say

_____

_____

_____

_____

_____

_____

_____

Name: Date:

Using Punctuation

Language Literacy Lessons / Writing Elementary
Copyright ©2002 by Incentive Publications, Inc.
Nashville, TN.

Bonita's Story

Bonita loves to write stories.

Her classmates say she is the best storywriter in the class.

Her one problem is that she forgets the punctuation marks.

Without punctuation marks, her stories are hard to read.

Help Bonita out by putting the punctuation marks and capital letters where they belong.

Then give the story a name.

Title:

_____

Jack fell asleep on the cool green grassy lawn beside the pond he forgot all about the big brown dog that lived there as he dreamed of far away places and strange and exciting events the dog stood patiently watching him from a distance it was only when the buzzing bumble bee began to circle Jack's nose that the dog moved closer when the bumble bee landed on Jack's nose the dog began to bark and jump around excitedly What do you think Jack's first thought was when he awoke to feel a bee on his nose and to see a big brown dog barking loudly beside him

Name: _____

Date: _____

Language Literacy Lessons / Writing Elementary
Copyright ©2002 by Incentive Publications, Inc.
Nashville, TN.

Punctuation (Capitalization, Titles)

Moonlight Makeover

Read the groups of words. If the words form a sentence, place the correct punctuation mark at the end.

If the group of words forms a phrase, go on to the next group.

Color the spaces in the puzzle that show the numbers of sentences.

Do not color the spaces that show the numbers of phrases.

1. The moon gives light at night
2. A full moon
3. The moon moves around the earth
4. One bright night
5. The moon's trip around the earth takes four weeks

6. Have you ever seen a full moon
7. In the shining moonlight
8. In the morning
9. Wasn't it a beautiful night
10. As bright as day

Name:

Date:

Sentences

Language Literacy Lessons / Writing Elementary
Copyright ©2002 by Incentive Publications, Inc.
Nashville, TN.

My Favorite Animal

A **declarative** sentence states a fact. A period comes at the end of it.

An **imperative** sentence gives a command, and a period comes at the end of it, too.

An **interrogative** sentence asks a question and has a question mark at the end of it.

An **exclamatory** sentence expresses strong feelings or emotions, and an exclamation point comes at the end of it.

1. Write a declarative sentence to tell about your favorite animal.

_____

_____

2. Write an interrogative sentence to ask a friend what his or her favorite animal is.

_____

_____

3. Write an imperative sentence giving a command to an animal.

_____

_____

4. Write an exclamatory sentence praising the animal for obeying your command.

_____

_____

Name: _____   Date: _____   (29)

Signs and Sentences

Explain these signs to someone who speaks
a language other than your own.

Write a complete sentence to tell
what each of the signs means.

1. _____
   _____
   _____

2. _____
   _____
   _____

3. _____
   _____
   _____

4. _____
   _____
   _____

Name: _____ Date: _____

Declarative Sentence

Language Literacy Lessons / Writing Elementary
Copyright ©2002 by Incentive Publications, Inc.
Nashville, TN.

Earthly Delights

Separate each of the following run-on sentences to make 2 complete sentences.

Place a period at the end of each sentence.

Capitalize the first word of the second sentence.

1. Earthworms are content in the earth it is dark and damp

   _____

   _____

2. They do not like sunlight they do not like dry dirt

   _____

   _____

3. Earthworms dig their burrows by eating the earth they digest it as they crawl

   _____

   _____

4. Their burrows bring air to the roots of plants this air aids the plant's growth

   _____

   _____

5. Common enemies of the earthworm are the robin and the mole the centipede and the platypus are enemies too

   _____

   _____

Name: _____   Date: _____   (31)

Correcting Run-on Sentences

Four Birthdays a Year

Birthdays are quite fun, but unfortunately they come only once a year on Earth. That's because it takes Earth 365 days to make one revolution around the sun. If you could fly to the planet Mercury, you could have 4 birthdays in one Earth year; Mercury's year is one fourth the time of an Earth year because it takes only 88 Earth days for Mercury to revolve around the sun.

If you could have 4 birthdays a year ...

1. Write a sentence to tell how you would spend your winter birthday.

   _____

2. Write a sentence to tell how you would spend your spring birthday.

   _____

3. Write a sentence to tell how you would spend your summer birthday.

   _____

4. Write a sentence to tell how you would spend your fall birthday.

   _____

5. Write a sentence to tell how you would ask a friend to come to your birthday party.

   _____

6. Write a sentence to tell how you would react if you received a surprise birthday gift.

   _____

   _____

   _____

   _____

Name: _____   Date: _____

Writing a Variety of Sentences

Language Literacy Lessons / Writing Elementary
Copyright ©2002 by Incentive Publications, Inc.
Nashville, TN.

The Big Discovery

Write a complete sentence to tell what you would do in each of the following situations.

1. You find an elephant on your back porch

_____

_____

_____

2. After you give him some food, he sits down in your mother's lounge chair

_____

_____

_____

3. He falls asleep and begins to snore very loudly

_____

_____

4. The neighbor's dog runs over barking

_____

_____

5. Your mother comes out to ask what is happening

_____

_____

Name: _____   Date: _____

Language Literacy Lessons / Writing Elementary
Copyright ©2002 by Incentive Publications, Inc.
Nashville, TN.

Writing Sentences in Sequence

Caps for Thinkers

When someone tells you to "put on your thinking cap," he or she usually means for you to think very hard about a particular thing.

Design a "thinking cap" for each of these thinkers.

Beside each thinker, write a sentence telling one particularly important thing that this thinker might need to think hard about.

Remember to use the correct punctuation marks.

Weasel

King of the Trolls

Ship Captain

You

Name: _____

Date: _____

Using Punctuation Marks

Language Literacy Lessons / Writing Elementary
Copyright ©2002 by Incentive Publications, Inc.
Nashville, TN.

A Lucky Ending

Number the sentences below to show the order in which they occurred.

Then rewrite the sentences in paragraph form on the lines below.

Don't forget to indent and use correct punctuation.

____ The spectators watched in wonder to see what would happen next.

____ Then all of a sudden, one of the engines stopped.

____ The plane hovered for a few seconds then started dropping quickly.

____ The plane taxied down the runway and slowly went up into the sky.

____ They were relieved to see the pilot and copilot parachute to the ground safely.

_____

_____

_____

_____

_____

_____

_____

_____

_____

Name: _____   Date: _____

Language Literacy Lessons / Writing Elementary
Copyright ©2002 by Incentive Publications, Inc.
Nashville, TN.

Sequencing Ideas

Add the Missing Details

Write a paragraph telling the story you see in this picture.

_____

_____

_____

_____

_____

_____

Study the picture carefully, and draw in details to make the scene show a very exciting event.

Now, look at your completed masterpiece, and write the new story it tells.

(Use the back of your paper for your new story.)

Name: _____   Date: _____

Writing a Descriptive Paragraph

Language Literacy Lessons / Writing Elementary
Copyright ©2002 by Incentive Publications, Inc.
Nashville, TN.

Whose School?

Brandon thinks students have more fun than teachers. He says that teachers have to come to school earlier and stay later than kids.

Marilou thinks teachers make all the rules and have more freedom to do as they choose. She says that teachers come to school because they want to and kids come because they have to.

Do you agree with Brandon or with Marilou?

Write a paragraph telling what you think.

Check your work for correct spelling and punctuation.

_____

_____

_____

_____

_____

_____

_____

_____

_____

_____

_____

_____

Name: _____   Date: _____

Language Literacy Lessons / Writing Elementary
Copyright ©2002 by Incentive Publications, Inc.
Nashville, TN.

Writing an Expressive Paragraph

Change Over

Think of something you would like to change about your life.

Then write a paragraph to tell how you could begin to make that change.

Name:

Date:

Writing a Personal Paragraph

Language Literacy Lessons / Writing Elementary
Copyright ©2002 by Incentive Publications, Inc.
Nashville, TN.

Select Your Topic

Select one of the topics below and write a paragraph about it.

Remember to indent and check your work for correct punctuation.

My Teacher!

Our Best Trip!

My Pet!

What I Like About My Teacher

The Best Trip I've Ever Taken

A Pet I Would Like To Own

Name: _____

Date: _____

Writing a Personal Paragraph

Daily Fare

Pandas at the National Zoo in Washington, D.C. are fed the following diet twice a day:

MENU:

carrots	sweet potatoes	bamboo	vitamins
apples	rice mixed with milk	dog biscuits	honey sandwiches

Write a paragraph to tell about feeding time for the pandas. Use resources from the library for additional information if you need it.

_____

_____

_____

_____

_____

_____

_____

_____

_____

_____

_____

_____

_____

Writing an Informative Paragraph

Language Literacy Lessons / Writing Elementary
Copyright ©2002 by Incentive Publications, Inc.
Nashville, TN.

Flying High

Look at this picture carefully.

Write a paragraph to tell what will happen next.

_____

_____

_____

_____

_____

_____

_____

Name: _____   Date: _____

Writing an Imaginative Paragraph

Catalog Capers

Many people order clothes by mail instead of shopping in stores.

The companies that sell the clothes mail catalogs with pictures and short descriptions of the items. People look at the pictures and read the descriptions, then decide what to buy.

For each catalog item below, write a short description that will make a person want to order it.

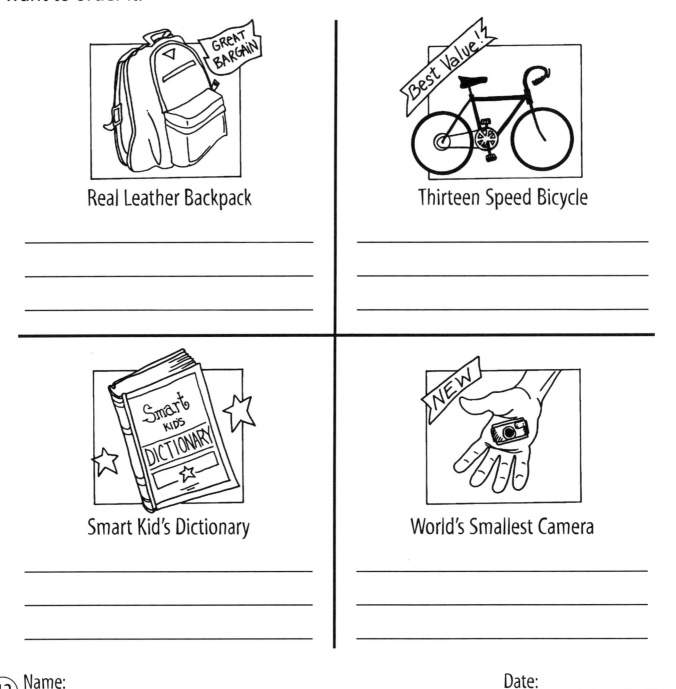

Real Leather Backpack

Thirteen Speed Bicycle

Smart Kid's Dictionary

World's Smallest Camera

Name:

Date:

Writing a Descriptive Paragraph

Language Literacy Lessons / Writing Elementary
Copyright ©2002 by Incentive Publications, Inc.
Nashville, TN.

Composition
and
Creative Writing

The Big Game

Read the paragraph below.

Then design a poster to advertise the game.

Be sure that the poster includes the who, what, when, and where.

The Fast Runners softball team will play the Great Hitters team at two o'clock in the afternoon on Monday, June 29. Tickets will cost $1.00 for adults and $0.50 for children under 12. The game will take place at City Road Park on 79th Street.

Name: _____

Date: _____

Who, What, Where, When, and Why

Language Literacy Lessons / Writing Elementary
Copyright ©2002 by Incentive Publications, Inc.
Nashville, TN.

Biographical Interview

Interview a classmate.

Fill out this biographical data sheet to gather information to use to write the person's biography.

Remember, a biography must include facts, not fiction.

Name_____

Parents' Names _____

_____

Date of Birth _____

Place of Birth _____

Weight and Length at Birth _____

Favorite Things (*sport, toy, song, TV program, foods*)

_____

_____

_____

_____

Names and Ages of Brothers and/or Sisters

_____

_____

_____

_____

Special Talents _____

_____

Three Wishes _____

_____

_____

Other Important Facts _____

_____

_____

Name:_____ Date:_____

Language Literacy Lessons / Writing Elementary
Copyright ©2002 by Incentive Publications, Inc.
Nashville, TN.

Writing Biographical Information

An Interesting Life Story

Use the information gathered on the biographical interview sheet to write a biography.

A **biography** must be a true account of the person's life. The writer can add interest by including the most exciting events and by using colorful and creative words and sentences. Use the back of the sheet if you need more room to complete your biography.

LAKE and CITY News 75¢

VOL. 30 ISSUE 19
Thursday, June 13, 2002

Lower Housing Taxes .... p. 4
Summer Magic! .... p. 6
Birthday Fun .... p. 11

An Interesting Life!

A biography of _____

by _____

_____

_____

_____

_____

_____

_____

Language Literacy Lessons / Writing Elementary
Copyright ©2002 by Incentive Publications, Inc.
Nashville, TN.

Tell it Like it Is

An **autobiography** is the story of one person's life, written by that person.

An autobiography includes facts about time and place of birth, family, schools attended, and places lived. A good autobiography also includes things of interest such as hobbies, friends, funny incidents, likes, dislikes, and dreams for the future.

Write your autobiography here.

FOREST and TOWN News 75¢

VOL. 20 ISSUE 11
Tuesday, April 16, 2002

Wilderness Fire . . . . p. 2
Spring Blooms . . . . p. 5
Zoo Babies . . . . p. 10

My Remarkable Life!

An autobiography of _____

_____

_____

_____

_____

_____

_____

_____

Name: _____

Date: _____

Writing an Autobiography

The Perfect Birthday Gift

Have you ever wrapped a birthday gift?

It is a step-by-step task.

Here are the steps for wrapping a gift.

The steps are mixed up.

Read all the steps first.

Then place the steps in correct order by numbering them 1–10.

____ Tie a bow at the top of the gift.

____ Cut the amount of paper you will need.

____ Gather together the gift box, tape, wrapping paper, scissors, ribbon or yarn, and a gift card.

____ The gift is ready to give!

____ Place the box on the wrapping paper. Estimate how much paper you will need.

____ Fill out the gift card and tape it under the bow.

____ Fold the paper together at each side. Place a piece of tape on each side.

____ Pull ribbon or yarn around the box. Allow extra ribbon for a bow. Cut as much ribbon as you think you will need.

____ Place the gift box face-down on the wrapping paper. Pull the paper together at the top. Place a piece of tape there.

____ Turn the wrapped gift so the box is face-up. The seam of the wrapping paper will be at the bottom.

Name: _____

Date: _____

Sequencing/ Writing Directions

Language Literacy Lessons / Writing Elementary
Copyright ©2002 by Incentive Publications, Inc.
Nashville, TN.

Question Time

You are usually asked to write answers to questions.

This time, you write the questions.

1. Question: _____

   _____

   Answer: A big fat hen

2. Question: _____

   _____

   Answer: Money

3. Question: _____

   _____

   Answer: A rocking rabbit

4. Question: _____

   _____

   Answer: Mealtime magic

5. Question: _____

   _____

   Answer: Over the rainbow

6. Question: _____

   _____

   Answer: A hungry cowboy

Name: _____   Date: _____   ⑨49

Writing Questions

Where in the World?

Imagine that you were walking down the main street of your town early on a Sunday morning, when suddenly a huge bird swooped down from behind a cloud, picked you up and soared into the sky.

After a flight that seemed endless, the bird deposited you on a strange planet and disappeared. As you looked around you saw the scene above.

What in the world would you do?

How would you find out where you were and how to get back to earth?

Write five good questions that you would want to ask.

Since you are limited to five, you should word each question carefully.

1. _____ ?

2. _____ ?

3. _____ ?

4. _____ ?

5. _____ ?

Name: _____ Date: _____

Writing Questions

Language Literacy Lessons / Writing Elementary
Copyright ©2002 by Incentive Publications, Inc.
Nashville, TN.

Riddle Zoo

Read and solve the animal riddles.

Then write a 4-line riddle for one other animal from the Riddle Zoo.

Maybe I live in the jungle
Or in a circus or a zoo,
But I carry my own trunk
Wherever I go
I am an _____

I have spots all over
And long, skinny legs
A pain in my neck
Is a long, long pain.
I am a _____

_____

_____

_____

_____

I am _____

Name: _____

Writing Riddles

Write a Letter

Select one of the following letters to write. Write it in the space below.

__ A letter from Goldilocks to Baby Bear, apologizing for breaking his chair

__ Snow White's farewell letter to the dwarfs

__ Cinderella's letter to her stepmother, written a week after her marriage to the prince

Dear _____

☆ Yours truly, _____

A Better Letter

Select a country that you would like to know more about. Write a letter to a boy or girl in that country. Tell the person about your school and your teacher.

Then ask your pen pal three questions about his or her school.

Remember ...   • The heading gives your address and the date.
                • The greeting tells who will receive the letter.
                • The body carries your message.
                • The closing is a sign-off from you.
                • The signature gives your name.

Name: _____   Date: _____   53

Product Progress

Look around your room and find 2 products that were not in use 10 years ago. Write the name of each of the objects.

1. _____

2. _____

Now think of 2 products that could be designed for use during the next 10 years. Try to be as creative as possible and think of products that would be exciting as well as useful. Name your products and write a short description of each.

1. (name) _____

_____

_____

_____

2. (name) _____

_____

_____

_____

_____

Name: _____

Date: _____

Imaginative Writing

Language Literacy Lessons / Writing Elementary
Copyright ©2002 by Incentive Publications, Inc.
Nashville, TN.

Cookie Jar

Write the conversation that is taking place.

Then draw a panel to show what will happen next.

Writing Dialogue/ Predicting Outcomes

Elephants Don't Make Good Pets

Write the conversation that is taking place.

Write three sentences or fewer to tell what will happen next.

_____

_____

_____

_____

_____

_____

Name: _____ Date: _____

Writing Dialogue/Predicting Outcomes

The Other Side of It

Write the other half of each conversation in the correct balloon.

Finger Talk

Finish each finger puppet below.

Write a puppet play for the characters you have created.

Then cut out the puppets and present your play.

_____

_____

_____

_____

_____

_____

_____

_____

_____

Name: _____   Date: _____

| Writing a Play |

Language Literacy Lessons / Writing Elementary
Copyright ©2002 by Incentive Publications, Inc.
Nashville, TN.

Rhyme Time

Draw lines to connect the rhyming words.

Then use the words to write rhyming couplets.

goat frown
can bed
cat pan
red coat
brown hat

1. The funny old <u>goat</u>
   Is wearing a new <u>coat</u>.

2. _____

   _____

3. _____

   _____

4. _____

   _____

5. _____

   _____

Name: _____

Date: _____

Language Literacy Lessons / Writing Elementary
Copyright ©2002 by Incentive Publications, Inc.
Nashville, TN.

Writing Rhyming Couplets

Poet at Work

Pick up your pencil and

Open your mind.

Each boy and girl can

Make poems that rhyme.

This fun poetry is called an **acrostic**.

The word that the poem tells about is written vertically down the left-hand side of the paper, and each line across begins with one of the word's letters.

Write an acrostic in the box below.

Writing an Acrostic

Language Literacy Lessons / Writing Elementary
Copyright ©2002 by Incentive Publications, Inc.
Nashville, TN.

Select a Season

Use your crayons to make this beautiful picture show one of the seasons of the year. Select your colors carefully to represent fall, winter, spring, or summer.

Write a haiku to express the beauty of your colored landscape.

Remember, a **haiku** is unrhymed and has three lines.

Lines 1 and 3 must have 5 syllables each. Line 2 must have 7 syllables.

A **haiku** usually refers to one of the four seasons.

_____

_____

_____

Name: _____

Date: _____

Language Literacy Lessons / Writing Elementary
Copyright ©2002 by Incentive Publications, Inc.
Nashville, TN.

Writing Haiku

I Like You

Design an "I Like You Because …" poster for one of your favorite people.

Draw pictures and write three complete sentences to make your poster show at least three things that you especially like about this person.

Try to blend the words you use into the overall design of your poster.

Use crayons or colored markers to create extra excitement.

Name: _____

Date: _____

Creating a Poster

Language Literacy Lessons / Writing Elementary
Copyright ©2002 by Incentive Publications, Inc.
Nashville, TN.

Sentence Selection

Read the words in the columns below.

Write 4 sentences using one word or phrase from each column.

Use all the words and phrases.

I	II	III
The good ship Lollipop	landed	in space
The trained astronaut	orbited	for final inspection
The earth person	reported	on a strange planet
Satellite II	awaited	an unexpected crater

1. _____

_____

2. _____

_____

3. _____

_____

4. _____

_____

Language Literacy Lessons / Writing Elementary
Copyright ©2002 by Incentive Publications, Inc.
Nashville, TN.

Developing Writing Flexibility

Puzzle It Out

To solve this puzzle:

   1. Cross out the letter A.

   2. Cross out the letter J.

   3. Cross out the letter S.

   4. Cross out the letter T.

   5. Cross out the next to last letter of the alphabet.

Write the message:

_____

_____

G	O	A	O
D	W	J	O
R	K	P	U
S	Z	Z	T
L	E	L	O
Y	V	E	R

Make your own puzzle. Write the directions for solving the puzzle and ask a friend to solve it.

1. _____

2. _____

3. _____

4. _____

5. _____

6. _____

7. _____

_____

Name: _____

Date: _____

Writing Simple Directions

Language Literacy Lessons / Writing Elementary
Copyright ©2002 by Incentive Publications, Inc.
Nashville, TN.

MAKE A THING

Can you use the tools and materials pictured here to construct a useful object?

Draw a picture to show how the completed object will look.

Give it a name and tell what it will be used for.

Now, write step-by-step directions for its construction.

Name: _____

Date: _____

Writing Sequenced Directions

Souvenir Special

Collecting souvenirs is a favorite hobby for people of all ages. Vacation trips, carnival outings, and even shopping sprees encourage otherwise conservative shoppers to spend money for either serious or silly souvenirs.

List 3 of the most unusual souvenirs you have bought (or that have been given to you), and tell where they were found.

Souvenir	From
1. _____	_____
2. _____	_____
3. _____	_____

How would you like to be the chief souvenir designer for your hometown?

Design the one souvenir you would want to be manufactured and sold to represent your hometown to the rest of the world.

Will it be a doll, a pennant, a book, a postcard, a T-shirt, or ...?

Show a detailed drawing of the souvenir, and provide a written description and suggested price for it.

WOW! WHAT A SOUVENIR!

Name: _____

Date: _____

Writing a Product Description

Language Literacy Lessons / Writing Elementary
Copyright ©2002 by Incentive Publications, Inc.
Nashville, TN.

Farmer Frank's Folly

Poor Farmer Frank! He has so many things to think about. When he hurried away from the barnyard this morning, he forgot to finish some of his jobs.

Find and circle six things that could cause trouble before the day is over.

On a piece of paper, write a story about something that happened on Farmer Frank's farm because of his carelessness. Give your story a beginning to make the reader want to read it, a middle that tells the story, and an exciting ending.

Name: _____   Date: _____

Language Literacy Lessons / Writing Elementary   *Developing Plot and Sequence*
Copyright ©2002 by Incentive Publications, Inc.
Nashville, TN.

Just Suppose

Just suppose that …

      * you could pay a visit to the country of your choice

      * you found a baby dinosaur on your school playground

      * a spaceship landed in your bedroom

      * there were no clocks anywhere in the world

Choose one of the "just suppose" ideas listed above.

Write a story about it.

_____

_____

_____

_____

_____

_____

_____

_____

_____

_____

_____

   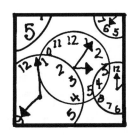

Name: _____

Date: _____

| Writing an Imaginative Story |

Ready for Takeoff

Place your fist in the box below and trace around it with your pencil.

Add features to make a spacecraft.

Then write a description of the spacecraft. Use resources from the library to learn more about space traveling if you need to. Then, write a good paragraph telling about the journey.

Spacecraft Description

_____

_____

_____

Name: _____   Date: _____

Developing a Fictional Paragraph

Look into the Crystal Ball

Look at this picture that appeared in the crystal ball.

Use your crayons or markers to color and add whatever you wish to make it more exciting.

Look at the new picture you have created.

Write the story it tells here.

_____

_____

_____

_____

Name: _____ Date: _____

Using Picture Clues to Develop a Story

The Rocking Chair Mystery

Who is this gentleman?

Where did he come from? Why is he sitting here?

Write his life story.

Name: _____

Date: _____

Language Literacy Lessons / Writing Elementary
Copyright ©2002 by Incentive Publications, Inc.
Nashville, TN.

Creating a Character

A Family's Story

Imagine that a family of 6 (a mother, a father, a grandfather, a girl, a boy, and a tiny baby girl) live in a house. Add a pet, a broken-down old car, a nosy next-door neighbor, and a singing mailman.

Now, write the story of what happened inside the house during the year.

Finish drawing in details to make the picture help tell the story you write.

Name: Date:

Developing a Story Based on Characters

Language Literacy Lessons / Writing Elementary
Copyright ©2002 by Incentive Publications, Inc.
Nashville, TN.

Animal Antics

Draw in the missing parts for the animals above.

Make each one a "never seen before" imaginative creature.

Then draw in a background.

Name the animals and write a mystery story about an adventure the animals might have.

_____

_____

_____

_____

_____

_____

_____

Name: _____   Date: _____   (73)

Writing a Mystery Story

Write the Story

Select one of these titles for the picture above:

* An Upside-Down Day

* A Funny Forest

* An Animal Mix-Up

Write a story to go with it.

_____

_____

_____

_____

_____

_____

_____

Developing a Story from a Main Idea

Language Literacy Lessons / Writing Elementary
Copyright ©2002 by Incentive Publications, Inc.
Nashville, TN.

A Storm at Sea

Read the beginning of the story about the great storm at sea.

Then finish the story with a surprise ending that will make others want to read it.

The clouds grew darker and darker. The sun completely disappeared from the sky. Even though it was only 12 o'clock noon, the sky quickly became as dark as midnight. Thunder roared and lightning flashed. Sheets of rain, mixed with hail, beat against the ship's hull. The ship rocked from side to side as the waves rolled higher and higher. In spite of the captain's best efforts, members of the ship's crew became more and more frightened. Then, the strangest thing happened. Suddenly. . .

_____

_____

_____

_____

_____

_____

_____

_____

_____

_____

_____

Name: Date:

Language Literacy Lessons / Writing Elementary
Copyright ©2002 by Incentive Publications, Inc.
Nashville, TN.

Finishing a Story

What If . . . Story Starters

What if . . .
- all the mud in the world turned into ice cream?
- a band of wandering gnomes came to your town?
- all the world's pencils and pens suddenly disappeared?
- horses were required to wear sunglasses?

Select one of the above "What If's" to use as a theme for a creative short story. Be sure to give your story an exciting climax. (Use the back of your paper for more room to finish your story.)

_____

_____

_____

_____

_____

_____

_____

_____

The Last Night at Sea

Tonight is the last night of a long journey. Tomorrow, the ship will dock in its home port.

The cabin boy is having a silly dream.

Draw the boy's dream in the dream bubble.

Then, write the dream on another sheet of paper.

Name: _____

Writing an Imaginative Piece

Answer Key

Page 14

Crocuses	Irises	Poppies
Roses	Lilacs	Lilies
Tulips	Orchids	Pansies
Daisies	Violets	

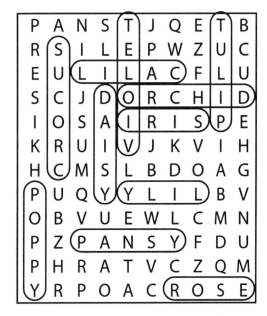

Page 16

Words that can be both a noun and a verb:

Wax	Pan	Fall
Stuff	Wish	Slip
Play	Cook	Train
Trip	Fly	

Page 17

finally	first	last
cheerfully	next	excitedly
happily	carefully	gleefully

Page 21

1. son, sun
2. eight, ate
3. see, sea
4. tale, tail
5. one, won,
   wait, weight

Page 22

evening
country
dark
quiet
black

Page 24

Gen.	= General
Capt.	= Captain
No.	= number
a.m.	= morning
Tues.	= Tuesday
Mar.	= March
St.	= Saint
Ave.	= Avenue
TX	= Texas
ft.	= feet
hr.	= hour
min.	= minutes
p.m.	= evening

Page 26

Once upon a time, long, long ago, a wooly white lamb was owned by a little girl named Mary. The lamb had a very bad habit of following Mary to school each day. To tell the truth, Mary liked having the lamb at school, but the teacher had a different opinion.

"Oh, no, not again!" the teacher would say. "Mary, why did you bring that lamb to school?"

"Please, teacher," Mary would say,
(Remaining answers will vary)

Language Literacy Lessons / Writing Elementary
Copyright ©2002 by Incentive Publications, Inc.
Nashville, TN.

Answer Key

Page 27

Jack fell asleep on the cool green grassy lawn beside the pond. He forgot all about the big brown dog that lived there. As he dreamed of faraway places and strange and exciting events, the dog stood patiently watching him from a distance. It was only when the buzzing bumble bee began to circle Jack's nose that the dog moved closer. When the bumble bee landed on Jack's nose, the dog began to bark and jump around excitedly. What do you think Jack's first thought was when he awoke to feel a bee on his nose and to see a big brown dog barking loudly beside him?

Page 28

Numbers 1, 3, 5, 6, and 9 are complete sentences.

Page 31

1. Earthworms are content in the earth. It is dark and damp.
2. They do not like sunlight. They do not like dryness.
3. Earthworms dig their burrows by eating the earth. They digest it as they crawl.
4. Their burrows bring air to the roots of plants. This aids the plant's growth.
5. Common enemies of the earthworm are the robin and mole. The centipede and platypus are enemies, too.

Page 35

<u>4</u> The spectators watched in wonder to see what would happen next.

<u>2</u> Then all of a sudden, one of the engines stopped.

<u>3</u> The plane hovered for a few seconds, then started dropping quickly.

<u>1</u> The plane taxied down the runway and slowly went up into the sky.

<u>5</u> They were relieved to see the pilot and copilot parachute to the ground safely.

Page 48

<u>8</u> Tie a bow at the top of the gift.

<u>3</u> Cut the amount of paper you will need.

<u>1</u> Gather together the gift box, tape, wrapping paper, scissors, ribbon or yarn, and a gift card.

<u>10</u> The gift is ready to give!

<u>2</u> Place the box on the wrapping paper. Estimate how much paper you will need.

<u>9</u> Fill out the gift card and tape it under the bow.

<u>5</u> Fold the paper together at each side. Place a piece of tape on each side.

<u>7</u> Pull ribbon or yarn around the box. Allow extra ribbon for a bow. Cut as much ribbon as you think you will need.

<u>4</u> Place the gift box face-down on the wrapping paper. Pull the paper together at the top. Place a piece of tape there.

<u>6</u> Turn the wrapped gift so the box is face-up. The seam of the wrapping paper will be at the bottom.

Page 51

1. Elephant
2. Giraffe

Page 59

1. goat, coat
2. can, pan
3. cat, hat
4. red, bed
5. brown, frown

Page 64

Good Work Puzzle Lover

Language Literacy Lessons / Writing Elementary
Copyright ©2002 by Incentive Publications, Inc.
Nashville, TN.